KS2 English Reading
Comprehension

This brilliant CGP Targeted Question Book is perfect for pupils who are ready for an extra challenge in Year 3 Reading Comprehension.

It's jam-packed with a huge range of tricky fiction, non-fiction and poetry texts, chosen from a wide range of authors and genres to really stretch the most confident readers.

And there's more! We've included plenty of practice questions, tailored to support the National Curriculum and develop pupils' reading skills. You'll find full answers to every question at the back. Enjoy!

What CGP is all about

Our sole aim here at CGP is to produce the highest quality books — carefully written, immaculately presented and dangerously close to being funny.

Then we work our socks off to get them out to you — at the cheapest possible prices.

p.2: Extract from *Cyborg Cat and the Night Spider*. Text copyright © Ade Adepitan 2019. First published in the UK by Piccadilly Press, an imprint of Bonnier books Ltd.

p.6: The abridged extract from *Little House in the Big Woods* by Laura Ingalls Wilder is used with the permission of Little House Heritage Trust, the copyright owner. All rights reserved.

p.8: Abridged extract from *Man Climbs Hong Kong Skyscraper in Wheelchair*. © NewsForKids.net. Used with permission.

p.10: Extract from *Ash Mistry and the Savage Fortress*. Reprinted by permission of HarperCollins Publishers Ltd © 2011 Sarwat Chadda.

p.14: Abridged extract from Jane Goodall Interview from National Geographic Kids UK, published by Creature Media.

p.18: Abridged extract from *Teen's round-the-world yacht Wild Eyes found floating eight years after boat abandoned*. Copyright Guardian News & Media Ltd 2019.

p.26: Extract from *Black and British: A Short, Essential History*, first published in 2020 by Macmillan Children's Books an imprint of Pan Macmillan. Reproduced by permission of Macmillan Publishers International Limited. Text copyright © David Olusoga.

p.28: Abridged extract from *The Piemakers* by Helen Cresswell (Copyright © Helen Cresswell). Reprinted by permission of A M Heath & Co. Ltd. Authors' Agents.

A note for teachers, parents and caregivers
Just something to bear in mind if you're choosing further reading for Year 3 pupils — all the extracts in this book are suitable for children of this age, but we can't vouch for the full texts they're taken from, or other works by the same authors.

Published by CGP

Editors: Alex Fairer, Catherine Heygate, James Summersgill
Contributors: Alison Griffin, Louise McEvoy

With thanks to Andy Cashmore and Lucy Towle for the proofreading.
With thanks to Lottie Edwards for the copyright research.

ISBN: 978 1 78908 350 7

Printed by Elanders Ltd, Newcastle upon Tyne.
Illustrations on cover and pages 16, 24 and 37 © Katy Nicholson

Text, design, layout and original illustrations © Coordination Group Publications Ltd. (CGP) 2021
All rights reserved.

Photocopying this book is not permitted, even if you have a CLA licence.
Extra copies are available from CGP with next day delivery. • 0800 1712 712 • www.cgpbooks.co.uk

Contents

Cyborg Cat and the Night Spider 2
Fiction by Ade Adepitan

Great White Sharks 4
Non-fiction by Melissa Gardner

Little House in the Big Woods 6
Classic fiction by Laura Ingalls Wilder

Wheelchair Skyscraper Climb 8
News article from www.newsforkids.net

Ash Mistry and the Savage Fortress 10
Fiction by Sarwat Chadda

My Shadow 12
Classic poetry by Robert Louis Stevenson

An Interview with Dr Jane Goodall 14
Non-fiction from www.natgeokids.com

Five Children and It 16
Classic fiction by Edith Nesbit

Wild Eyes 18
News article from www.theguardian.com

Poems about Bedtime 20
Poetry by Andy Cashmore and Margaret Thomson Janvier

Odysseus and Circe 22
Myth by Melissa Gardner

The Princess and the Goblin 24
Classic fiction by George MacDonald

Black and British 26
Non-fiction by David Olusoga

The Piemakers 28
Fiction by Helen Cresswell

Stories of Great Inventors 30
Biography by Hattie E. Macomber

Answers 32

Cyborg Cat and the Night Spider

This extract is from a book by Ade Adepitan, a successful wheelchair basketball player and TV presenter. Like the main character in the book, he was born in Nigeria and caught polio when he was a baby. He works to encourage more people with disabilities to get into sport.

"**WHAT** a save!"

"Incredible!"

"Cyborg* Cat is taking his game to superhuman levels! How does he do it?"

My goalkeeping that day was pretty good, if I do say so myself. The Parsons Road Gang was
5   playing football after school. I was in goal against Dexter, Melody, Shed and Brian, and I'd saved just about every one of their shots. Maybe it was because I was in a really good mood — we'd just found out that we were going on a school trip to a safari park. Or perhaps my cyborg skills were growing. Either way, I was on blistering form.

"Your super-cyborg leg was practically glowing when you made that last save," Dexter
10   shouted, wide-eyed and out of breath.

"I'm telling you, the caliper* is the source of his powers," Brian said seriously.

The gang looked in awe at the metal scaffolding surrounding my left leg. I'd contracted polio* in Nigeria when I was little, which made my leg weak, so it was there to help me walk. But it had earned me the nickname Cyborg Cat amongst my friends because I could do cool moves
15   no one ever expected. The element of surprise was my secret weapon on the football pitch.

"Er, guys!" I said, feeling a little awkward. "I'm still here, you know. I can actually hear what you're saying."

"Sorry, Ade, but we're never going to score against you today," said Shed. "I reckon even a team of animals from the safari park wouldn't be able to get a goal past the Cyborg Cat."

20   That got me thinking.

What a pass by Lenny Lion, straight to Eric Elephant, who controls the ball and back-heels it to Terry Tiger. Terry beats one beast, beats two, beats a third and sends in a beautiful cross. Geoffrey Giraffe out-jumps
25   the defenders and heads it perfectly... it must be a goal, surely... but no! Cyborg Cat launches himself through the air, stretches out and somehow tips the ball over the bar. How did he do that? He must have super-powers!

Glossary
cyborg — a person who is part human and part machine
caliper — a metal frame used to support someone's leg
polio — a disease that can cause muscle weakness

An extract from *Cyborg Cat and the Night Spider* by Ade Adepitan.

1) How is the person in line 1 speaking? How can you tell?

....
....
2 marks

2) Ade thinks he is playing well. What two reasons does he give for why he's playing well?

....
....
2 marks

3) What does Ade mean when he says he feels "a little awkward" (line 16)? Why does he feel like this?

....
....
2 marks

4) Do you like the description of the football match in lines 21-28? Why or why not?

....
....
....
2 marks

5) Line 28 says that Cyborg Cat "must have super-powers". How does this link back to the first three lines of the extract?

....
....
2 marks

Total = /10

Extra Activities

- Do you think "Cyborg Cat" is a good nickname for Ade? Why or why not? Discuss your thoughts with a partner.

- Ade Adepitan creates an imaginative scene in the last paragraph. Write your own short description of animals playing a sport and then draw a picture of the scene.

- Write a short story about yourself with a super-power. What would your super-power be? What would you call yourself? What would you do with your super-power?

© Not to be photocopied   Year 3 Stretch — Targeted Comprehension

Great White Sharks

There are many different types of shark in our seas. The smallest is about the size of a human hand, but when people think of sharks, they usually think of the biggest and the most feared shark — the great white shark. This text asks just how scary great whites really are...

Great white sharks have a fearsome reputation. They are powerful hunters with huge bodies and razor-sharp teeth. It's no wonder people find them threatening. But are they really as dangerous to humans as people imagine?
5 We take a close look at these mighty predators to find out.

Excellent Hunters

Great white sharks have fantastic senses, which makes catching dinner a breeze. Their superb vision and their sharp hearing lets them seek out their prey from a distance. They can detect the scent of other animals from a long way away too — they can even
10 sniff out small amounts of blood in the water, which allows them to find wounded prey.

These sharks are also surprisingly stealthy. You might think that their size — female great whites can sometimes reach lengths of 6 metres — would give them a disadvantage in sneaking up on their prey. Not so! Great white sharks attack their prey from below. They can also reach speeds of more than 20 mph, which, combined with
15 the angle of their attack, makes it hard for their prey to see them coming. This allows the shark to grab a bite out of its meal with its staggeringly powerful jaws.

Shark Attacks

Although great white sharks have occasionally been known to attack humans in the water, they do not in fact hunt humans. The great white shark's vicious reputation is
20 largely a result of how they are shown in films, on television and in newspapers. Most attacks on humans that do take place are not deadly. As great white sharks tend to deliver one swift bite and then retreat while their prey weakens, humans who are bitten often have time to escape and seek medical attention.

So what do these sharks hunt? Most of the time, they
25 survive on large fish (e.g. tuna, swordfish and rays), sea turtles, dolphins, seals and sea lions. Scientists think that most attacks on humans happen when sharks mistake humans for their natural prey. Their advice? Don't wear jewellery, light or bright colours in the water,
30 as these can attract a shark's attention. Also, don't surf in areas where sharks have been sighted, as they have been known to mistake surfboards for seals.

By Melissa Gardner.

1 Write down a word that the author could have used instead of "fearsome" (line 1).

....
1 mark

2 Name three things that make it easier for great white sharks to find their prey.

....
1 mark

3 Why do great white sharks approach their prey from below?

....

....
2 marks

4 Does the text argue that sharks are more or less dangerous to humans than people think? Explain your answer.

....

....

....
3 marks

5 Why do you think this text might have been written?

....

....

....
3 marks

Total = /10

Extra Activities

- What do you think about great white sharks after reading this extract? Do you feel afraid of them? Why or why not? Discuss your thoughts with a partner.

- Make a poster that tells people about great white shark attacks. Explain how likely it is that they will be attacked by a great white shark and what they can do to make an attack less likely. Use as much information from the text as possible.

- Write a short story about someone who comes across a great white shark while they are swimming in the sea. What do they do when they spot it? What happens next?

Little House in the Big Woods

Little House in the Big Woods is a novel by Laura Ingalls Wilder. Set in 1871, it is based on Laura's memories of growing up in Wisconsin, America. Laura's family were pioneers — pioneers were people who travelled to the west of America to settle and develop new land there.

Very early one morning Pa strapped the bundle of furs on his shoulders, and started to walk to town. There were so many furs to carry that he could not take his gun.

Ma was worried, but Pa said that by starting before sun-up and walking very fast all day he could get home again before dark.

5   The nearest town was far away. Laura and Mary had never seen a town. They had never seen a store. They had never seen even two houses standing together. But they knew that in a town there were many houses, and a store full of candy and calico* and other wonderful things — powder*, and shot*, and salt, and store sugar.

The sun sank out of sight, the woods grew dark, and he did not come. Ma started supper
10 and set the table, but he did not come. It was time to do the chores, and still he had not come.

Ma said that Laura might come with her while she milked the cow. Laura could carry the lantern. [...]

When Laura walked behind Ma on the path to the barn, the little bits of candle-light from the lantern leaped all around her on the snow. The night was not yet quite dark. The woods
15 were dark, but there was a grey light on the snowy path, and in the sky there were a few faint stars. The stars did not look as warm and bright as the little lights that came from the lantern.

Laura was surprised to see the dark shape of Sukey, the brown cow, standing at the barnyard gate. Ma was surprised, too.

It was too early in the spring for Sukey to be let out in the Big Woods to eat grass. She
20 lived in the barn. But sometimes on warm days Pa left the door of her stall open so she could come into the barnyard. Now Ma and Laura saw her behind the bars, waiting for them.

Ma went up to the gate, and pushed against it to open it. But it did not open very far, because there was Sukey, standing against it. Ma said,

"Sukey, get over!" She reached across the gate and slapped Sukey's shoulder.

25 Just then one of the dancing little bits of light from the lantern jumped between the bars of the gate, and Laura saw long, shaggy, black fur, and two little, glittering eyes.

Sukey had thin, short, brown fur. Sukey had large, gentle eyes.

Ma said, "Laura, walk back to the house."

So Laura turned around and began to walk toward the house.
30 Ma came behind her. When they had gone part way, Ma snatched her up, lantern and all, and ran. Ma ran with her into the house, and slammed the door.

Then Laura said, "Ma, was it a bear?"

"Yes, Laura," Ma said. "It was a bear."

An abridged extract from *Little House in the Big Woods* by Laura Ingalls Wilder.

Glossary		
calico — a type of cotton fabric	powder — gunpowder	shot — gun bullets

① How do you think Laura and Mary feel about the town?

....
....

2 marks

② Why do you think the author repeats the phrase "not come" in lines 9-10?

....
....

2 marks

③ Why do you think the author compares what "Laura saw" to what "Sukey had" in lines 26-27?

....
....

2 marks

④ How do you think Ma feels in lines 28-32? Explain your answer.

....
....

2 marks

⑤ Would you like to live far away from towns and other houses like Laura does? Why or why not?

....
....

2 marks

Total = /10

Extra Activities

- Imagine that you are out for a walk and you come face-to-face with a bear. How do you think you would feel? What do you think you would do? Discuss your thoughts with a partner.

- Imagine that you are Laura. Write a diary entry covering the events of this extract. Describe how you felt when Pa was late coming home, when you realised that the animal in the barnyard wasn't Sukey, and when you got back into the house.

- Continue writing the story to show what you think might happen next. What does the bear do? How do Ma, Laura and Mary deal with the bear? Does Pa come home?

Wheelchair Skyscraper Climb

This article is about Lai Chi-wai, a Hong Kong climber who uses a wheelchair. In January 2021, he made headlines across the world when he attempted to climb a skyscraper using only his arms and a rope system. Strong winds and tangled ropes made the climb even more difficult...

Man Climbs Hong Kong Skyscraper in Wheelchair

Last Saturday, Lai Chi-wai used a rope system to pull himself up over 820 feet (250 meters) along the side of a skyscraper in Hong Kong. Mr. Lai, who can't move his legs, was strapped into his wheelchair as he climbed.

Before 2011, Mr. Lai was a world-famous rock climber. He was ranked eighth in the world, and had won the Asian Rock Climbing Championship four times. He also taught others how to climb.

That ended 10 years ago, when Mr. Lai was involved in a car crash. The accident left him paralyzed from the waist down, unable to move his legs. Since then, he's needed to use a wheelchair to get around.

But Mr. Lai couldn't get over his love of climbing. He figured out a way to attach his wheelchair to a roping system that allowed him to climb again. He began working as a climbing teacher once more.

In 2016, Mr. Lai climbed Lion Rock in Kowloon, Hong Kong. It's a 1,624-foot (495-meter) climb that he had done many times before his accident.

Mr. Lai said climbing Lion Rock again made him realize that he could still climb successfully, even if he couldn't do it in the same way he had in the past. "In a way, I forgot that I was a disabled person, I could still dream and I could still do what I liked doing," he said.

Last Saturday, Mr. Lai hoped to pull himself up 1,050 feet (320 meters) to the top of Hong Kong's Nina Tower. It was a very different challenge from climbing Lion Rock.

Nina Tower (centre) is one of the tallest buildings in Hong Kong.

"Climbing up a mountain, I can hold onto rocks or little holes," Mr. Lai said, "But with glass, all I can really rely on is the rope that I'm hanging off." […]

Finally, after climbing for 10 hours and reaching a height of about 820 feet (250 meters), the winds became too rough, and Mr. Lai had to give up his goal of reaching the top.

But along the way, he set a new record. He also raised over $700,000 for a charity that is working to help others who have been paralyzed.

Mr. Lai said that often, disabled people are viewed as weak. He hoped his climb would send a different message. "If a disabled person can shine," he said, "They can at the same time bring about opportunity, hope, bring about light, they don't have to be viewed as weak."

An abridged article from www.newsforkids.net

① What evidence is there in lines 6-10 that Lai Chi-wai was a successful climber?

....

....

2 marks

② Read lines 16-20. Do you think Lai Chi-wai sounds like a determined person? Explain your answer.

....

....

2 marks

③ Find and copy the word that means the same as 'depend' in lines 36-39.

....

1 mark

④ How do you think Lai Chi-wai might have felt after having to stop the climb early? Why do you think this?

....

....

2 marks

⑤ Why do you think Lai Chi-wai attempted to climb Nina Tower? Give three reasons.

....

....

....

3 marks

Total = /10

Extra Activities

- Do you think that Lai Chi-wai is an inspirational person? Discuss your thoughts with a partner.

- Imagine you have achieved something impressive, like Lai Chi-wai climbing the skyscraper. You might have won a sports competition or done something challenging to raise money for charity. Write a news article reporting your achievement. Make sure the article explains who you are and what you did.

- Write a letter to Lai Chi-wai telling him what you think of the article. In the letter, ask him five questions about his life or the skyscraper climb which you want to know the answer to.

Ash Mistry and the Savage Fortress

Ash Mistry and the Savage Fortress is by Sarwat Chadda, a British author who has a south-Asian Muslim background. The book was inspired by Sarwat's travels to India, which is where the story is set. This extract from the first chapter introduces the main character Ash and his sister, Lucky.

"That is *so* not a cobra," said Ash. It couldn't be. Weren't cobras endangered*? You couldn't have them as pets, not even here in India.

"That so totally *is* a cobra. Look," said his sister, Lucky.

Ash leaned closer to the snake. It swayed in front of him, gently gliding back and forth
5   in tempo* with the snake charmer's flute music. The scales, oily green and black, shone in the intense sunlight. It blinked slowly, watching Ash with its bright emerald eyes.

"Trust me, Lucks," said Ash. "That is not a cobra."

The snake revealed its hood*.

It was, totally, a cobra.

10   "Told you," she said.

If there was anything worse than a smug sister it was a smug sister three years younger than you.

"What I meant was, of course it's a cobra, but not a real cobra," replied Ash, determined his sister wasn't going to win this argument. "It's been defanged. They all are. Hardly a cobra at all. More like a worm with scales."

15   Almost as though it had been following the conversation, the cobra hissed loudly and revealed a pair of long, needle-sharp ivory fangs.

Lucky waved at it.

"I wouldn't do that if —"

The cobra darted at Lucky and before Ash knew it he'd jumped between them. The snake's
20   mouth widened and he stared at the two crystal drops of venom* hanging off its fangs.

"Parvati!" snapped the snake charmer. The cobra stopped a few centimetres from Ash's neck.

Whoa.

The snake charmer tapped the basket with his flute and the cobra, after giving Ash one last look, curled itself back into it and the lid went on.

25   Ash started breathing again. He looked at Lucky. "You OK?"

She nodded.

"See that? I just saved your life," Ash said. "I practically *hurled* myself between you and that incredibly poisonous snake. Epically brave." And, now the heart palpitations* had subsided*, epically stupid. But protecting his little sister was his duty in the same way hers was to cause as
30   much trouble as possible.

An extract from *Ash Mistry and the Savage Fortress* by Sarwat Chadda.

Glossary

endangered — at risk of dying out	in tempo — in time	hood — the wide part of a cobra's neck
venom — poison	palpitations — rapid beats	subsided — decreased

1 Do lines 4-6 make it easy to imagine what the snake looks like? Explain your answer.

....

....

2 marks

2 What makes Ash and Lucky realise that the snake is definitely a cobra?

....

1 mark

3 Why does Ash call the snake a "worm with scales" (line 14)?

....

....

2 marks

4 Read lines 15-24. Does the cobra seem well trained? Explain your answer.

....

....

2 marks

5 How do you think Ash feels in lines 27-30? Explain your answer.

....

....

....

3 marks

Total = /10

Extra Activities

- Do you think that Ash was "brave" (line 28) or "stupid" (line 29) in this extract? Discuss your thoughts with a partner.

- Look back at the author's description of the snake in lines 4-6. Write your own description of an animal. What does it look like and how does it behave?

- Rewrite the extract from the snake's point of view. What does the snake think about the children? How does it feel when the children talk about it? How does it feel when it goes back into its basket?

© Not to be photocopied   Year 3 Stretch — Targeted Comprehension

My Shadow

Robert Louis Stevenson was born in Edinburgh, Scotland in 1850. He wrote novels, short stories and poems during his career as a writer. His poem *My Shadow* is about a child who doesn't understand what a shadow is. Shadows are formed when a solid object blocks out light.

I have a little shadow that goes in and out with me,
And what can be the use of him is more than I can see.
He is very, very like me from the heels up to the head;
And I see him jump before me, when I jump into my bed.

5 The funniest thing about him is the way he likes to grow —
Not at all like proper children, which is always very slow;
For he sometimes shoots up taller like an india-rubber* ball,
And he sometimes gets so little that there's none of him at all.

He hasn't got a notion of how children ought to play,
10 And can only make a fool of me in every sort of way.
He stays so close beside me, he's a coward you can see;
I'd think shame to stick to nursie* as that shadow sticks to me!

One morning, very early, before the sun was up,
I rose and found the shining dew on every buttercup;
15 But my lazy little shadow, like an arrant* sleepy-head,
Had stayed at home behind me and was fast asleep in bed.

Robert Louis Stevenson

Glossary

india-rubber — a type of rubber

to stick to nursie — to stay close to his childminder

arrant — absolute

1) What are the two pairs of words that rhyme in the first verse?

....

2 marks

2) Explain how the narrator's shadow grows differently to the way children grow.

....

....

2 marks

3) Find and copy the word that means the same as 'idea' in the third verse.

....

1 mark

4) Why does the narrator think his shadow isn't with him in the fourth verse? What is the real reason his shadow isn't there?

....

....

2 marks

5) What do you think the narrator thinks about his shadow? Explain your answer.

....

....

....

3 marks

Total = /10

Extra Activities

- Do you like this poem? Why or why not? Discuss your thoughts with a partner.
- This poem uses pairs of rhyming words. Write down one more word to rhyme with each pair of rhyming words in the poem.
- Imagine what your shadow would say if it could speak. What sort of personality do you think it might have? Write a paragraph from your shadow's point of view.
- Draw the shadow doing one of the things that the narrator describes in this poem. Write the part of the poem that you have illustrated next to your drawing.

An Interview with Dr Jane Goodall

Dr Jane Goodall is a famous primatologist, which means that she studies primates like chimpanzees. Goodall was the first person to study chimpanzees in the wild. This led to some exciting discoveries, which she speaks about in this interview with National Geographic Kids...

NGK: Hi Jane, when did you first know you wanted to work with animals?

Jane: I was **ten** when I decided I wanted to go to Africa and **live with wild animals** and **write books** about them. That's about **70 years ago** now, and back then **girls** in England **didn't have those opportunities**. So everybody laughed at me and said, "Jane, dream about something you can achieve."

But my mother said, "If you really want something, you're going to have to **work hard**, take advantage of every **opportunity** and never give up!"

NGK: Great advice! What's been special about the work you've done?

Jane: I studied animals differently from other people. While I was in **Gombe, Tanzania** in the 1960s, other scientists told me I'd done my whole study of chimpanzees wrong — that **I shouldn't** have given the chimps **names**, that they should've been **numbered**, because that's scientific. I was told I couldn't talk about their **personalities**, **minds** or **emotions** — because they thought those things were unique to* humans. But luckily, I'd learned from my **dog** as a child, that that was **rubbish**!

NGK: Sounds like having a childhood pet really helped you in your studies! What are you most proud of?

Jane: Helping people to understand — thanks to the chimps — that **humans** are part of the **animal kingdom**, not separate from it. When I started out, nobody else was studying chimps in the wild, so I was able to show how their behaviour is like ours — **kissing**, **cuddling**, **holding hands**, **patting** one another, **reassurance** etc. [...]

NGK: What surprised you most about the chimps?

Jane: Sadly, they're capable of a type of **war** — they can be **violent** and **aggressive**. But they also show **love**, **compassion** and **care** for others.

NGK: What memories do you have of chimps caring for each other?

Jane: I remember a little three-year-old male chimp called **Mel** who was **orphaned** after his mother died. Mel was just beginning to eat solid foods, and so he'd reached an age where he could *theoretically* * survive without his mother. Unfortunately, his survival seemed unlikely as he didn't have an older **brother** or **sister** to care for him — which is what would normally happen. But to our amazement, a **12-year-old unrelated male** called **Spindle** adopted him! He **carried him around** on his back, **rescued him** from difficult situations, reached out and **took him into his nest** at night, **shared his food** with him. Spindle completely saved the little orphan's life!

It was the first time I'd seen that with unrelated chimps. It was very moving because Spindle had just **lost his own mother**, so it was almost like this little infant had helped him get over *his* grief.

An abridged extract from www.natgeokids.com

Glossary
unique to — only found in
theoretically — possibly

① Why do you think that some words in Jane Goodall's answers are in bold?

....
....
2 marks

② Did Jane Goodall's mother support her dream of studying wild animals when she was a child? Explain your answer.

....
....
2 marks

③ Did other scientists approve of Jane Goodall's work? Why or why not?

....
....
2 marks

④ In your own words, explain why Jane Goodall's work shows that "humans are part of the animal kingdom" (lines 16-17).

....
....
2 marks

⑤ How do you think Jane Goodall feels about chimps? Explain your answer.

....
....
....
2 marks

Total = /10

Extra Activities

- Make a poster celebrating the achievements of Jane Goodall. Explain what she does, what she has discovered and why she is important.

- Write a short story about the chimps, Mel and Spindle, that Jane talks about in her last answer. Describe how they meet, what makes Spindle decide to look after Mel, and how Spindle rescues Mel from a "difficult" (line 31) situation.

- Imagine you are going on a research trip to study a type of animal. Write a paragraph explaining what animal you are studying, what you want to find out about it, and how you might try to do this.

Five Children and It

Five Children and It is a novel by Edith Nesbit. It tells the story of five siblings who meet a strange creature while playing outside. The creature grants the children wishes, which never quite go to plan. In this extract, the children meet the creature for the first time...

The children stood round the hole in a ring, looking at the creature they had found. It was worth looking at. Its eyes were on long horns like a snail's eyes, and it could move them in and out like telescopes; it had ears like a bat's ears, and its tubby body was shaped like a spider's and covered
5   with thick soft fur; its legs and arms were furry too, and it had hands and feet like a monkey's.

"What on earth is it?" Jane said. "Shall we take it home?"

The thing turned its long eyes to look at her, and said —

"Does she always talk nonsense, or is it only the rubbish
10 on her head that makes her silly?"

It looked scornfully at Jane's hat as it spoke.

"She doesn't mean to be silly," Anthea said gently; "we none of us do, whatever you may think! Don't be frightened; we don't want to hurt you, you know."

"Hurt *me*!" it said. "*Me* frightened? Upon my word! Why, you talk as if I were nobody in particular."
15 All its fur stood out like a cat's when it is going to fight.

"Well," said Anthea, still kindly, "perhaps if we knew who you are in particular we could think of something to say that wouldn't make you angry. Everything we've said so far seems to have done so. Who are you? And don't get angry! Because really we don't know."

"You don't know?" it said. "Well, I knew the world had changed — but — well, really — Do you
20 mean to tell me seriously you don't know a Psammead when you see one?"

"A Sammyadd? That's Greek to me*."

"So it is to everyone," said the creature sharply. "Well, in plain English, then, a *Sand-fairy*. Don't you know a Sand-fairy when you see one?"

It looked so grieved* and hurt that Jane hastened* to say, "Of course I see you are, *now*. It's quite
25 plain now one comes to look at you."

"You came to look at me, several sentences ago," it said crossly, beginning to curl up again in the sand.

"Oh — don't go away again! Do talk some more," Robert cried. "I didn't know you were a Sand-fairy, but I knew directly I saw you that you were much the wonderfullest thing I'd ever seen."

The Sand-fairy seemed a shade less disagreeable after this.

An extract from *Five Children and It* by Edith Nesbit.

Glossary
That's Greek to me — I don't understand that word
grieved — upset   hastened — rushed

1) Explain how the children react to the Sand-fairy and why.

....
....
....

2 marks

2) Explain how the Sand-fairy reacts to the children and why.

....
....

2 marks

3) Do you think that Jane really does realise that the creature is a Sand-fairy in lines 24-25? Explain your answer.

....
....

2 marks

4) How do you think the Sand-fairy feels at the end of the extract? Explain your answer.

....
....
....

2 marks

5) What do you think of the Sand-fairy's behaviour in this extract?

....
....
....

2 marks

Total = /10

Extra Activities

- Read the introduction to the extract. Imagine you meet the Sand-fairy. Write a short story describing what wish you make and what happens when your wish is granted.

- Draw a picture of your own strange creature that is made up of parts of other animals like the Sand-fairy is. Write a description of your creature next to your picture.

- Create a leaflet to explain to people what a Sand-fairy is. Include a description of what Sand-fairies look like and warn people how they should behave if they ever meet one.

Wild Eyes

In 2010, Abby Sunderland attempted to become the youngest person to sail around the world on their own. However, her attempt ended when she had to be rescued from her yacht in bad weather. This article reveals what happened to her yacht, which was abandoned in the ocean...

Teen's round-the-world yacht Wild Eyes found floating eight years after boat abandoned

Yacht spotted near Kangaroo Island off South Australian coast after being abandoned by 16-year-old sailor Abby Sunderland in 2010.

Eight and a half years after it was abandoned in the middle of the Indian Ocean when 16-year-old solo sailor Abby Sunderland had to be rescued in rough seas, a yellow yacht named Wild Eyes has been found floating upside down off the coast of South Australia.

The 40-foot yacht was encrusted* with barnacles*, the signature eyes on the hull* scratched and faded. Its mast snapped off in the wild weather that forced Sunderland's rescue midway through her world record attempt to be the youngest solo sailor to circumnavigate* the globe in 2010.

Sunderland, who said she saw the footage of the rediscovered yacht on the news, said she was "very emotional".

"My heart skipped a beat," she said in a statement. "It brought back many memories — good and not so good — but it was neat to see it after so long. It looked a little creepy but that's to be expected after so long." [...]

Sunderland, now 25, set sail from Marina del Rey in California on 23 January in 2010 but had to restart her world record attempt at Cabo San Lucas in Mexico 10 days later due to electrical problems and higher-than-expected fuel and power use from her navigation and communication systems.

Her family had bought the Australian-built Wild Eyes in October the year before, just months after her elder brother Zach became the first person under the age of 18 to sail solo around the world, with stops and assistance, and kitted it out specifically for her journey. [...]

Sunderland intended to beat her brother's record and complete a non-stop circumnavigation, but had to stop in Cape Town for repairs in May. She activated her emergency satellite beacons after being tumbled about in 60-knot winds and 50-foot waves about 2,000 miles east of Madagascar.

Her parents were heavily criticised for allowing her to undertake the attempt, and Sunderland in turn criticised the media saying that her age had nothing to do with encountering a storm in the southern ocean, something she said happened to all sailors.

An abridged extract from *www.theguardian.com*

Glossary
- encrusted — covered
- barnacles — a type of shellfish
- hull — main body of a boat
- circumnavigate — go all the way around

1) Why do you think Abby thought her yacht looked "a little creepy" (line 23)?

....
....

2 marks

2) Do you think Abby is happy that her yacht has been found? Explain your answer.

....
....

2 marks

3) What did Abby hope would make her trip around the world different from her brother Zach's?

....

1 mark

4) How do you think Abby's brother might have felt about her trying to beat his record?

....
....

2 marks

5) Why do you think Abby's parents were criticised for allowing her to try to sail around the world? Do you think they should have been criticised? Explain your answer.

....
....
....

3 marks

.... Total = /10

Extra Activities

- Would you like to sail around the world? Why or why not? What sort of challenges do you think someone sailing around the world might face? Discuss your thoughts with a partner.

- Imagine you are Abby Sunderland. Write a letter to a newspaper explaining why you think your parents were right to let you try to beat the world record.

- Write a paragraph about a world record you would like to achieve. Describe what your world record would be, why you have chosen it and what you would need to do to achieve it.

Poems about Bedtime

Dreaming Friend by Andy Cashmore is a poem about a young girl falling asleep with her cat. *The Sandman* by Margaret Thomson Janvier is based on the character of the Sandman, a man from old stories who sprinkles sand over children's eyes to bring them sleep and good dreams.

Dreaming Friend

Maha's eyes begin to droop,
When the night replaces day,
It's then her parents tell her,
"Off to bed, without delay."

5   Bitter moans and raging stomps,
Are heard going up the stairs,
But so are dainty* footsteps,
From soft paws as light as air.

Maha launches into bed,
10 Fighting calls to fall asleep,
When her warm companion
Joins her with a nimble* leap.

He nestles against her chin,
Soothes her with his silky fur,
15 And sends Maha off to sleep
To the sound of gentle purrs.

           Andy Cashmore

The Sandman (an extract)

The rosy clouds float overhead,
The sun is going down;
And now the sandman's gentle tread*
Comes stealing through the town.
5 "White sand, white sand," he softly cries,
And as he shakes his hand,
Straightway there lies on babies' eyes
His gift of shining sand.
Blue eyes, grey eyes, black eyes, and brown,
10 As shuts the rose, they softly close, when he
                          goes through the town.

So when you hear the sandman's song
Sound through the twilight sweet,
Be sure you do not keep him long
A-waiting in the street.
15 Lie softly down, dear little head,
Rest quiet, busy hands,
Till, by your bed his good-night said,
He strews* the shining sands.
Blue eyes, grey eyes, black eyes, and brown,
20 As shuts the rose, they softly close, when he
                          goes through the town.

           Margaret Thomson Janvier

Glossary

dainty — small and delicate   nimble — quick and light   tread — footsteps   strews — scatters

1 How are lines 1-2 of these two poems similar?

....

....
2 marks

2 How do you think Maha in *Dreaming Friend* feels about going to bed? Explain your answer.

....

....
2 marks

3 What are the cat's footsteps compared to in *Dreaming Friend*?
Why do you think the poet made this comparison?

....

....
2 marks

4 Why might parents read *The Sandman* to their young children? Explain your answer.

....

....
2 marks

5 Which of these poems do you prefer? Why?

....

....
2 marks

.... Total = /10

Extra Activities

- Look at *The Sandman* with a partner. Work together to see which lines rhyme in the first verse. Does the second verse follow the same pattern?

- Write your own poem about going to bed. Do you enjoy going to bed? Why or why not? Write your poem using the same rhyming pattern that is used in *Dreaming Friend*.

- Write a description of what you think the Sandman might look like. Remember to give him somewhere to carry his sand. Draw a picture of him next to your description.

© Not to be photocopied   Year 3 Stretch — Targeted Comprehension

Odysseus and Circe

This myth is based on a story in the *Odyssey*, a poem written more than 2500 years ago. The *Odyssey* tells the story of the hero Odysseus and his difficult journey across the sea. He is trying to return to his family in ancient Greece after fighting in a war a long way from home.

Odysseus and his companions had washed up on another island. Their never-ending journey home still wasn't over, and they were exhausted. As the sun set, most of them fell asleep on the cold, grainy sand. But Odysseus climbed the steep cliff behind the beach. When he reached the top, he saw smoke rising from the woods nearby.

5 The next morning, he divided his crew in half. The half led by Odysseus's second-in-command, Eurylochus, went into the woods to investigate the source of the smoke. Odysseus waited with the other half, guarding the boats on the shore.

For hours and hours, they waited. Eventually, a man came stumbling out of the woods. He was covered in dirt and weeping. As he came closer, they saw that it was Eurylochus.

10 "What happened?" asked Odysseus.

"It… it was terrible!" Eurylochus stuttered. "The smoke came from a chimney. The cottage looked so normal, just like any other house. But the creature that lived there…"

"Go on!" urged Odysseus.

"She was a witch," said Eurylochus, "a truly awful one named
15 Circe. She invited us in for food and drink. The others gladly accepted the offer: it's been so long since we ate a good meal. I suspected it might be a trap, so I hid instead. It's lucky I did, because there was some sort of magic potion in the food. As soon as the others ate it, they turned into pigs."

20 "Pigs?"

"Pigs!" he said. "Then she put them in her pigsty along with all her other pigs. As soon as she went back inside, I ran. Anyone would have done the same." He shivered at the memory.

Odysseus could hardly believe what he was hearing, but he knew he had to rescue his companions. He grabbed his sword, did his best to ignore his thumping heart and marched through the woods
25 towards Circe's cottage. Suddenly, Hermes, the messenger god, appeared in his path.

"What are you doing, Odysseus?" he asked. "You'll never defeat Circe by force. If you really want to save your friends, eat the leaves of this plant. It's called *moly* and it will stop Circe's evil potion from working. Then, when you've beaten her magic, make Circe promise not to harm you."

Odysseus thanked Hermes and did exactly as he told him. When Circe invited him into her house,
30 he ate and drank without any fear. The *moly* leaves stopped the potion from having any effect. Circe was shocked and frightened: it seemed as though Odysseus had powers even greater than her own.

Fearing for her life, she immediately swore not to hurt him and promised to turn his companions back into men. Better still, she knew a lot about the seas nearby and offered him help with his journey. Odysseus smiled — maybe he and his crew might get home after all.

By Melissa Gardner.

1) What does the word "exhausted" (line 2) mean?

....

1 mark

2) Why do you think Odysseus wanted to investigate where the smoke was coming from?

....

....

2 marks

3) How do lines 8-9 make the reader feel? Explain your answer.

....

....

2 marks

4) How do you think Eurylochus felt about his companions being turned into pigs? How can you tell?

....

....

2 marks

5) Explain how you think Odysseus's emotions change between lines 23-34.

....

....

....

3 marks

Total = /10

Extra Activities

- Do you think Odysseus behaves like a hero in this story? Why or why not? Discuss your thoughts with a partner.

- Imagine that Odysseus and his crew stop on another island during their journey home. Write a short story describing where they stop and who or what they find there.

- Write a description of an imaginary plant that can do something special, like *moly* can in this story. Draw a picture of your plant beside your description and label its special features.

The Princess and the Goblin

The Princess and the Goblin is a novel by George MacDonald which was published in 1872. It tells the story of Princess Irene. Irene lives in a distant castle with her nursemaid, Lootie, who looks after her. In this extract, Lootie tries to persuade Irene to turn back after a long walk.

At length she observed that the sun was getting low, and said it was time to be going back. She made the remark again and again, but, every time, the princess begged her to go on just a little farther and a little farther; reminding her that it was much easier to go downhill, and saying that when they did turn they would be at home in a moment. So on and on they did go, now to look at a group of ferns over whose tops a stream was pouring
5   in a watery arch, now to pick a shining stone from a rock by the wayside, now to watch the flight of some bird. Suddenly the shadow of a great mountain peak came up from behind, and shot in front of them. When the nurse saw it, she started and shook, and catching hold of the princess's hand turned and began to run down the hill.

"What's all the haste, nursie?" asked Irene, running alongside of her.

"We must not be out a moment longer."

10   "But we can't help being out a good many moments longer."

It was too true. The nurse almost cried. They were much too far from home. It was against express orders to be out with the princess one moment after the sun was down; and they were nearly a mile up the mountain! If His Majesty, Irene's papa, were to hear of it, Lootie would certainly be dismissed; and to leave the princess would break her heart. It was no wonder she ran. But Irene was not in the least frightened, not knowing anything to be
15   frightened at. She kept on chattering as well as she could, but it was not easy.

"Lootie! Lootie! Why do you run so fast? It shakes my teeth when I talk."

"Then don't talk," said Lootie.

But the princess went on talking. She was always saying: 'Look, look, Lootie!' but Lootie paid no more heed to anything she said, only ran on.

20   "Look, look, Lootie! Don't you see that funny man peeping over the rock?"

Lootie only ran the faster. They had to pass the rock, and when they came nearer, the princess saw it was only a lump of the rock itself that she had taken
25   for a man.

"Look, look, Lootie! There's such a curious creature at the foot of that old tree. Look at it, Lootie! It's making faces at us, I do think."

Lootie gave a stifled cry, and ran faster still — so
30   fast that Irene's little legs could not keep up with her, and she fell with a crash. It was a hard downhill road, and she had been running very fast — so it was no wonder she began to cry. This put the nurse nearly beside herself; but all she could do was to run on, the
35   moment she got the princess on her feet again.

An extract from *The Princess and the Goblin* by George MacDonald.

1) What do lines 1-5 tell you about Lootie's character? Explain your answer.

....

....

....

2 marks

2) How does Lootie feel in lines 11-15? Explain your answer.

....

....

2 marks

3) Why is "shakes my teeth when I talk" (line 16) a good description?

....

....

2 marks

4) Do you think that Irene is brave in this extract? Explain your answer.

....

....

2 marks

5) What do you think will happen next? Explain your answer.

....

....

2 marks

.... Total = /10

Extra Activities

- Look back at your answer to question 5. Continue writing the story to show what you think might happen next.

- Write a paragraph describing how Irene's father, the king, reacts when he hears that Irene has been out so late. Describe how he feels about it and if he decides to punish Lootie.

- Design your own illustration for this extract. When you have finished, swap your illustration with a partner and explain why you have illustrated the extract the way that you have.

Black and British

Black and British is a history book written by David Olusoga. It is about the role of Black people throughout Britain's history — something which the author says he was never taught about in school. He describes this book as the book he wished he had been given at school.

Africans first came to Britain with the Roman Empire. Long before Britain began to build its own empire, it was invaded and conquered by the Romans in the year 43 AD. Britain became a region on the edge of the mighty empire of Rome, which stretched across Europe, North Africa and the Middle East.

5 When we talk about Romans, we don't just mean people from Rome or Italy. Roman citizens could come from anywhere in the empire. People from all over the empire and even beyond travelled huge distances to trade*, work, and fight in the Roman army. We know that Africans lived and settled in Roman Britain. By the time the Romans had been here for 200 years, some places in
10 Britain may even have had a more diverse population* than they do today.

Who were the Aurelian Moors?

The first recorded group of Africans living in Britain were soldiers in the Roman army. They came to defend the edge of the empire at Hadrian's Wall.

The wall stretched for more than seventy miles, right across what is now
15 northern England. It was built in the years after 120 AD by order of the Emperor Hadrian. He wanted a border for the empire in Britain, to control who could come in from the north and to defend against tribes who might attack. Soldiers were stationed in forts and watchtowers along the wall. Those soldiers came from all over the empire — and so did their families,
20 their commanders, and traders who sold them whatever they needed.

In 1934, Latin words were found carved into a stone in a village in Cumbria, north-west England. They said that a group of soldiers called the 'Aurelian Moors' had been stationed at the nearby fortress of Aballava between the years 253 and 258 AD. The word 'moors' means 'people from North Africa', the part of
25 the empire where the soldiers came from. They were named 'Aurelian' after the Emperor Marcus Aurelius. There is another mention of the Aurelian Moors of Aballava in a list of Roman officials' travel, which confirms that they were there.

An extract from *Black and British: A Short, Essential History* by David Olusoga.

Glossary
trade — buy or sell things

diverse population — a population that is made up of people from different cultures

1) Find and copy a word from lines 3-4 that shows the Roman Empire was powerful.

....

1 mark

2) Why does the author believe that Roman Britain may have had a diverse population?

....

1 mark

3) Why did the Emperor Hadrian build Hadrian's Wall? Give two reasons.

....

....

2 marks

4) Who were the Aurelian Moors? Where did the name 'Aurelian' come from?

....

....

2 marks

5) Read lines 21-27. How do we know the Aurelian Moors were in Britain? Give two reasons.

....

....

2 marks

6) Why might this text be useful to someone who wants to know more about history? Use the introduction to help you.

....

....

....

2 marks

Total = /10

Extra Activities

- Did you find this text interesting? Why or why not? Discuss your thoughts with a partner.
- Imagine you are interviewing an Aurelian Moor living in Roman Britain. What would you like to find out about them? Write down five questions you would ask them about their life.
- If you were going to write a non-fiction book, what would you like to write about? Write a paragraph to describe your book and explain why people should read it.

The Piemakers

Helen Cresswell's novel *The Piemakers* is about the Rollers, a family of piemakers from Danby Dale. In this extract, Arthy Roller has made a huge pie for the King's piemaking competition. Arthy's daughter Gravella is in the audience, hoping that their pie will impress the King...

Suddenly the crowd swayed and moved as if in a wind, and Gravella saw that the King was coming. He rode on a horse of pure white and banners of scarlet embroidered with gold fluttered round him. [...]

The notes of the bugles* went shining through the air and left behind them a silence
5   that only the skylarks did not mark. And, as always when there has been a great silence, no one dared to be the first to speak, and so the King and his party began to pass along the row of pies in silence. One by one they were tasted, a slice of each being placed on a golden plate and handed to the King, who tried a morsel*, neck arched, red comb* of hair flaming, like a cockerel, Gravella thought. Very very slowly, like a wave gathering,
10 first whispering, then murmuring, and then excited talking broke out among the crowd. Everyone strained to catch a glimpse of the King's face as he tasted, trying to read his judgement there. But he tasted the sixteenth pie and no one in the whole meadow dared guess the answer, and as he stood hesitating a great cry went up:

"The Danby Dale pie! Where's the Danby Dale pie!"

15 Delicately the King's eyebrows arched and the doors of the barn opened slowly on great groaning hinges. There was sudden silence. Out from the shadows came the huge pie-dish, wheeled by twenty men with straining shoulders. The sun fell for the first time on to that
20 glorious crust, perfectly smooth and brown, gleaming faintly. It was impossible, a miracle under that blue sky, standing among the grass and clover like some enormous fruit. It was seen and yet impossible to believe.

No one could speak for the wonder of it. Gravella could feel her own tongue
25 cleaving* to the roof of her mouth and her eyes stinging. Arthy was rigid, locked in awe. Though he had created it last night in the shadows of the barn, yet he could hardly believe it in the glare of sunlight. For a full minute the pie stood there and more than three thousand people stood and stared in silence, made into statues by their disbelief. Then the roar that broke out sent the skylarks somersaulting skyward and the din broke
30 in deafening fragments and Arthy was borne* up into the air and shouldered to the King.

An abridged extract from *The Piemakers* by Helen Cresswell.

Glossary
bugles — instruments like trumpets   morsel — small piece
comb — the red flesh on top of a chicken's head   cleaving — sticking   borne — lifted

① How does the author show that the King is important?

....
....
2 marks

② Why do you think the King hesitates after he has tried the sixteenth pie?

....
....
2 marks

③ Why is "groaning" (line 16) a good word to describe the noise of the hinges?

....
....
2 marks

④ How do the crowd feel when they first see Arthy's pie? Why do they feel like this?

....
....
2 marks

⑤ How do you think Arthy feels at the end of the extract? Explain your answer.

....
....
2 marks

.... Total = /10

Extra Activities

- Write a diary entry from Arthy's point of view about the night he created the pie. Was the pie difficult to make? How did he feel about the competition the next day?

- Continue writing the story to show what you think might happen next. What happened when Arthy reached the King? Did the King like Arthy's pie? Did Arthy's pie win the competition?

- Design a front cover for this book, using information from the extract and introduction. Your cover should show people what the book is about and help them to imagine the characters.

Stories of Great Inventors

James Watt was a Scottish engineer born in 1736. He made important improvements to the design of the steam engine, which became widely used in factories and mills. In this extract, written in America in 1897, the author imagines how James Watt came up with his ideas.

This story is about a giant. Do you believe in them? He peeps out of your coffee cup in the morning. He cheers you upon a cold day in winter. But the boys and girls were not so well acquainted* with him a hundred years ago. About that long ago, far to the north and east, a queer* boy lived. He sat in his grandmother's kitchen many an hour,
5 watching the tea-kettle. He seemed to be idle. But he was really very busy. He was talking very earnestly to the giant.

The giant was a prisoner. No one knew how to free him. Many had often tried to do this and failed. He was almost always invisible. But when he did appear, it was in the form of a very old man. This old man had long, white hair, and a beard which
10 seemed to enwrap him like a cloak — a cloak as white as snow. So his name is The White Giant.

The boy's name was James Watt. He lived in far-away Scotland. He sat long, listening to the White Giant as he told him many wonderful things. The way in which the giant first showed himself to James was very strange. James noticed that the lid of
15 the tea-kettle was acting very strangely. It rose and fell, fluttered and danced.

Now, James had lived all his life among people who believed in witches and fairies. So he was watching for them. And he thought there was somebody in the kettle trying to get out. So he said, "Who are you and what do you want?"

"Space, freedom, and something to do," cried the giant. "If you will only let me out, I'll
20 work hard for you. I'll draw your carriages and ships. I'll lift all your weights. I'll turn all the wheels of your factories. I'll be your servant always, in a thousand other ways."

If you have now guessed the common name of this giant, we will call him Steam.

At the time James Watt lived, there were no steam
25 boats, steam mills, nor railways. And this boy, though his grandmother scolded*, thought much about the giant in the tea-kettle. And he became the inventor of the first steam engine that was of any use to the world. So, little by little, people
30 came to know that steam is a great, good giant.

An extract from *Stories of Great Inventors* by Hattie E. Macomber.

Glossary
well acquainted — familiar queer — unusual scolded — told him off

① Why do you think the author describes steam as an old man (lines 9-10)?

....

....
2 marks

② Why do you think James Watt was told off by his grandmother (line 26)?

....

....
2 marks

③ Why is steam described as "a great, good giant" (line 30)?

....

....
2 marks

④ Write down an adjective to describe James's personality. Explain your choice.

....

....

....
2 marks

⑤ Why do you think the author doesn't reveal the giant's name straight away?

....

....
2 marks

.... Total = /10

Extra Activities

- Do you like the way the author describes steam in this extract? Do you like how she doesn't reveal that she is writing about steam straight away? Discuss your thoughts with a partner.

- Rewrite the extract from James Watt's point of view. Describe how he first noticed steam as a child and what he thought it was.

- What do you think is the best invention of all time? Create a poster with a drawing of this invention on it. On your poster, explain what the invention does and why you have chosen it.

Answers

How to mark your answers

- In this section, you'll find sample answers to all of the questions in this book.

- Many of the answers in this section start with "E.g.". This means that the question asked you to give your opinion or explain your own ideas about the text. There isn't one "correct answer" to these questions, and the answers we've given are only a guide. If you're unsure whether your answer is correct, you should ask a partner or teacher to look at your work.

- The more marks a question is worth, the more detailed your answer should be. For example, if a question is worth three marks, then you will need to make three separate points, or give three examples from the text.

Cyborg Cat and the Night Spider (pages 2-3)   **Author / Source:** Ade Adepitan   **Genre:** Fiction – novel extract

1. E.g. loudly; excitedly. Because the word "WHAT" is bigger than the rest of the text and is in bold.
2. E.g. He was in a good mood about going to a safari park. He thought that his cyborg skills might be growing.
3. E.g. That he feels uncomfortable and embarrassed. He feels like this because his friends are talking about him as if he isn't there.
4. E.g. Yes, because describing animals as footballers playing a match together is funny to imagine. It's also exciting, because it seems like Geoffrey Giraffe will score but then Cyborg Cat saves it.
5. E.g. At the start of the extract, it says that Ade is playing at a "superhuman" level, which suggests he has super-powers.

Great White Sharks (pages 4-5)   **Author / Source:** Melissa Gardner   **Genre:** Non-fiction – information text

1. E.g. terrifying; terrible; scary
2. E.g. Their excellent sight, hearing and sense of smell.
3. E.g. They are large creatures, but if they attack from below their prey might not see them, which means they can surprise them.
4. Less dangerous. E.g. The text says that sharks don't hunt humans, they only attack them by mistake. If you are attacked, sharks often bite and then retreat, which means you have a chance to escape and get help.
5. E.g. To help people learn about great white sharks and to show that they aren't as dangerous to humans as people might think. Also, to give people tips on how to avoid a shark attack.

Answers

Little House in the Big Woods (pages 6-7)   **Author / Source:** Laura Ingalls Wilder   **Genre:** Classic fiction – novel extract

1. E.g. I think they feel it's an exciting place because they think you can buy "wonderful" things there. They also might feel curious about it because they have never seen a town.
2. E.g. To show that it is getting later and later and still Pa has not come home. This makes you worry that something has happened to him.
3. E.g. To make you realise that the animal is not Sukey — the description of the animal's fur and eyes are very different to the description of Sukey's fur and eyes.
4. E.g. She seems terrified. She "snatched" Laura up, ran to the house and "slammed the door", which suggests she is scared of the bear and wants to get away from it.
5. E.g. No, because I think it might be quite lonely — you wouldn't see many people. It might also make life difficult because it would take a long time to travel to shops to get things you need. OR E.g. Yes, because I think it would be peaceful — it would be quiet and you would be surrounded by nature. I think it would also be fun, because there would be lots of space to play outdoors.

Wheelchair Skyscraper Climb (pages 8-9)   **Author / Source:** www.newsforkids.net   **Genre:** Non-fiction – news article

1. E.g. He was a "world-famous" climber. He also won four championships, which suggests he must have been really good at climbing.
2. E.g. Yes, because even though he was paralysed, he found a way to carry on doing the thing he loved, which must have taken hard work and determination.
3. "rely"
4. E.g. Disappointed, because he wanted to reach the top, but he also might have felt pleased that he set a new record and raised money.
5. E.g. He loves climbing so he probably enjoys trying new climbs. The climb raised money for charity, so he might have done it to help others. He might have also wanted to prove that disabled people can do amazing things.

Answers

Ash Mistry and the Savage Fortress (pages 10-11)
Author / Source: Sarwat Chadda
Genre: Fiction – novel extract

1. E.g. Yes, because descriptions like "green and black" and "bright emerald" help you to imagine the colours of the snake. "gently gliding" and "blinked slowly" help you to imagine how the snake moves.
2. The snake shows them its hood.
3. E.g. Because he thinks it has been "defanged", so it isn't dangerous. Worms don't have fangs, and they aren't dangerous. OR E.g. He wants to convince Lucky that it's not a real cobra because he really wants to win the argument.
4. E.g. Yes, because even though it tries to attack Ash and Lucky, it stops as soon as the snake charmer speaks. It also goes back into the basket when it is told to. OR E.g. No, because if it was well trained it wouldn't have tried to attack Ash and Lucky. It also gives Ash "one last look" before it goes into the basket, which might suggest it still wants to attack him.
5. E.g. He probably feels pleased with himself, because he says he was "Epically brave". He may also feel frightened by what he did though, because his actions are described as "epically stupid". He probably also feels relieved that he wasn't bitten by the snake.

My Shadow (pages 12-13)
Author / Source: Robert Louis Stevenson
Genre: Classic poetry

1. "me" and "see"; "head" and "bed"
2. E.g. Children slowly get taller, but the narrator's shadow grows tall very quickly and he can also get so short that you can't see him.
3. "notion"
4. E.g. He thinks his shadow has stayed in bed. The real reason is that the sun isn't up yet, so there's no light to make his shadow.
5. E.g. He thinks his shadow is useless because he wonders "what can be the use of him". He says that his shadow doesn't grow like "proper" children, which shows that he thinks his shadow is strange. He also thinks his shadow behaves badly, because he calls him a "coward" and "lazy".

An Interview with Dr Jane Goodall (pages 14-15)
Author / Source: www.natgeokids.com
Genre: Non-fiction – interview

1. E.g. To make them stand out. They are the most important words, so making them stand out helps you understand her answers better.
2. E.g. Yes, because her mother gave her advice to try and help her achieve her dream, like telling her to work hard and take advantage of opportunities.
3. E.g. No, because they thought she should have numbered the chimps rather than named them. They also said she couldn't talk about chimps having personalities, minds and emotions, because they thought that only humans have those things.
4. E.g. Because her work shows that humans and chimps behave in similar ways, which means that humans are part of the animal kingdom in the same way that chimps are.
5. E.g. She seems to find chimps interesting because she has studied them a lot. She also seems to be impressed by them, because she felt "amazement" when she saw how Spindle behaved towards Mel.

Answers

Five Children and It (pages 16-17)   **Author / Source:** Edith Nesbit   **Genre:** Classic fiction – novel extract

1. E.g. At first, they are confused because they don't know what sort of creature it is. When they see that it's annoyed by them, they speak "gently" and "kindly" to try and make sure they don't upset it any more.
2. E.g. It isn't very friendly to the children because it is annoyed and angry that they don't know who it is. It also doesn't like that they talk about taking it home.
3. E.g. No, she is just pretending because she has seen how "grieved and hurt" the Sand-fairy is because they don't know what it is.
4. E.g. I think it feels happier than it was before, because it seems to like how Robert calls it "the wonderfullest thing" he has ever seen — it is "less disagreeable" after this which means it isn't as mean.
5. E.g. I think the Sand-fairy was very rude to the children because it wasn't their fault they didn't know what it was — it's a really strange creature and they probably wouldn't have seen one before. OR E.g. I think the Sand-fairy was quite rude, but its behaviour was understandable because the children were rude too — they suggested taking it home as though it was a pet.

Wild Eyes (pages 18-19)   **Author / Source:** www.theguardian.com   **Genre:** Non-fiction – news article

1. E.g. Because it had been in the sea for such a long time — it was floating upside down and it had things growing on it so it probably didn't look very nice.
2. E.g. Yes, because it brought back good memories. Even though it brought back bad memories too, she said it was "neat" to see it which means she is pleased. OR E.g. No, because it brought back bad memories as well as good memories. She thought it looked a bit "creepy", so she might be wishing that she hadn't seen it again.
3. E.g. She wanted to do the trip without stopping.
4. E.g. He might have felt annoyed that she was trying to beat him. He might also have felt proud though, because she is his sister and he probably wanted her to do well.
5. E.g. Because people thought it was too dangerous for someone her age. AND E.g. Yes, they should have been criticised because it does seem like it was dangerous — the weather was bad and her mast broke, so it sounds like she could have been really hurt. OR E.g. No, they shouldn't have been criticised because I think it's good that they let her try to get the record — it sounds like a good challenge and an exciting adventure.

Answers

Poems about Bedtime
(pages 20-21)

Author / Source:
Andy Cashmore
Margaret Thomson Janvier

Genre:
Poetry

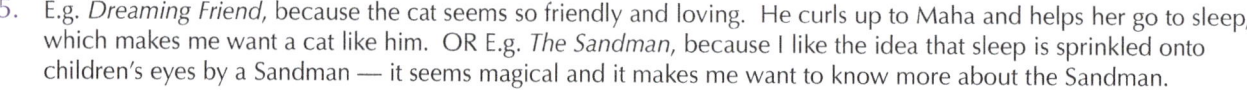

1. E.g. They show what time the poem is set — they both describe the day coming to an end which tells you that it's getting close to bedtime.
2. E.g. She seems annoyed about going to bed. She makes "Bitter moans and raging stomps" after being told to go to bed, which suggests she doesn't want to.
3. E.g. To air. To show how gently and quietly the cat goes upstairs.
4. E.g. To send them to sleep at bedtime — if children think that the Sandman is going to come and give them good dreams, it might encourage them to go to sleep.
5. E.g. *Dreaming Friend*, because the cat seems so friendly and loving. He curls up to Maha and helps her go to sleep, which makes me want a cat like him. OR E.g. *The Sandman*, because I like the idea that sleep is sprinkled onto children's eyes by a Sandman — it seems magical and it makes me want to know more about the Sandman.

Odysseus and Circe
(pages 22-23)

Author / Source:
Melissa Gardner

Genre:
Myth

1. E.g. very tired
2. E.g. Because the smoke is probably coming from a fire, which could mean that someone lives in the woods who might be able to help Odysseus and his crew with their journey.
3. E.g. These lines make the reader feel worried about Eurylochus and his men, because nothing happens for a long time and then Eurylochus comes back alone and crying.
4. E.g. I think he felt upset, because he was "weeping" when he reached Odysseus. He might also have been scared that Circe would turn him into a pig too, because he "ran" from her house.
5. E.g. At the start of these lines, he is shocked because he can "hardly believe" Eurylochus's story. He then feels nervous about having to go to Circe's house because his heart is "thumping". At the end of these lines, he "smiled", which shows that he is happy he might be able to get home.

Answers

The Princess and the Goblin (pages 24-25)

Author / Source: George MacDonald

Genre: Classic fiction – novel extract

1. E.g. These lines tell you that Lootie is the sort of person who wants to do the right thing, because she tries to turn back when she's supposed to. She isn't very strict though, because she keeps going when Irene begs her.
2. E.g. Lootie is really upset and worried — the extract says that she "almost cried", and she's scared that she'll lose her job.
3. E.g. It's a good description because it helps you imagine the sound and feeling of Irene's teeth as she talks, which shows you how fast they're running.
4. E.g. No, because when she falls over, she immediately starts crying. She also doesn't know that there's "anything to be frightened at", so she isn't really being brave. OR E.g. Yes, because she isn't afraid when she sees the rock that she thinks is a man or the "curious creature".
5. E.g. I think Irene will see the creature again. I think she'll get away from Lootie to investigate even though Lootie will tell her not to, because Irene seems interested by the creature and she doesn't really listen to Lootie in the extract.

Black and British (pages 26-27)

Author / Source: David Olusoga

Genre: Non-fiction – information text

1. "mighty"
2. E.g. Because the Romans came from many different places such as Europe, North Africa and the Middle East. OR Because Africans lived and settled in Roman Britain.
3. E.g. To control who came into the empire from the north and to help defend against attacking tribes.
4. E.g. They were soldiers from North Africa who were in the Roman army. 'Aurelian' came from the name of Emperor Marcus Aurelius.
5. E.g. Latin words that were written by Aurelian Moors were found carved into a stone in Cumbria and a list of Roman officials' travel mentions them.
6. E.g. Because it gives facts and information about the Romans and Black people in Britain. The introduction also says that this information wasn't taught to the author in school, so it might be something that a lot of people don't know about.

Answers

The Piemakers
(pages 28-29)

Author / Source: Helen Cresswell

Genre: Fiction – novel extract

1. E.g. He arrives on a horse, and he has scarlet and gold banners around him. He also seems important because people play bugles when he arrives.
2. E.g. Because he has to choose the winner of the pie-making competition, but he's still trying to decide which of the pies he has tasted is the best.
3. E.g. Because it helps you to imagine what sort of noise the hinges make. It also shows that the hinges are struggling, which tells you that the doors are big and heavy.
4. E.g. They feel amazed, because the pie is so big and looks so good that it seems like a "miracle" and is "impossible to believe".
5. E.g. He probably feels proud, because the crowd is impressed by the pie he has created. He is probably also nervous, because he can't be sure that the King will like his pie when he tastes it.

Stories of Great Inventors
(pages 30-31)

Author / Source: Hattie E. Macomber

Genre: Non-fiction – biography

1. E.g. Because steam is white and it swirls around, so you can imagine it looking like an old man who has "long, white hair" and a "beard" which wraps around him like a "cloak".
2. E.g. Because she thought he was sitting around doing nothing, when he was actually looking at and thinking about the steam.
3. E.g. It is "great" and a "giant" because it is very powerful compared to people. It is "good" because it can do things for people.
4. E.g. Curious, because he pays a lot of attention to the steam making the kettle lid go up and down. He even carries on thinking about the steam after his grandmother scolds him.
5. E.g. I think the author does this to make you want to read on to find out who the giant is. It also makes it more fun to read about James Watt, because it's like a puzzle you can try and solve.